QUESTIONS **20**

WHY DO ZEBRAS HAVE STRIPES?

By Gilda &
Melvin Berger

And **20** answers
about mammals

SCHOLASTIC INC.

ISBN 978-0-545-56323-9

12 11 10 9 8 7 6 5 4 3 2   13 14 15 16 17 18 /0

Printed in the U.S.A   40
First edition, September 2013
Book design by Kay Petronio

Q Why do giraffes have long necks?

Long necks help giraffes survive.

People used to believe that giraffes have long necks to reach high food and spot approaching **predators**. Though this is true, most scientists now think there is a third, even more important reason for their long necks. Male giraffes use their necks to fight other males, whipping their heads against and around the necks of their **rivals**. The giraffes with longer, stronger necks win the most attractive females.

Q

Are dolphins smart?

Yes, dolphins are nearly as smart as humans.

When compared, a dolphin's brainpower measures close to a human's. Like humans, dolphins use various sounds and body language to keep in touch with one another. A dolphin calf spends a long time with its mother, studying her ways and learning to copy her actions. Dolphins in aquariums and water shows are able to learn different performance skills, such as playing ball, jumping through hoops, painting, and "singing."

Q Why do zebras have stripes?

Stripes camouflage zebras.

Zebras often move in huge **herds** of a hundred or more animals. When closely packed and moving together, stripes make it difficult to tell one zebra from another. Lions—the zebra's biggest enemies—see them as one **mass** and cannot pick out a single animal to attack. Even when standing alone, stripes break up the outline of the zebra's body. Because lions are **color-blind**, the black and white stripes also help zebras to hide in green or brown grass.

Q Do horses sleep standing up?

9

Yes, horses often sleep while standing.

Actually, horses can sleep either standing up or lying down. But horses usually sleep standing up so that they can **flee** quickly, if necessary. Thanks to special "locks" in their knees, they can snooze on their feet without falling over. You may sometimes see horses lying down for a nap during the day. But look around. Very likely, nearby you'll spot a standing horse watching out for approaching danger.

Q What's in a camel's hump?

11

Camels store fat in their humps.

People used to think that camels' humps were filled with water. Now we know that the humps contain fat that camels use for energy when food is **scarce**. When the fat is all burned up, the empty humps hang loosely over the side of the camel's body. Experts think camels store fat in their humps and not all around their bodies, like other **mammals**, because the humps also help to protect the animals from the desert sun's very powerful heat.

Q

Why do cats purr?

Cats purr to communicate and to heal themselves.

Many people think that cats purr only when they are happy. But did you know that cats also purr when they're frightened or feel **threatened**? Perhaps you have heard or felt a cat purr when it was injured or in pain. The vibrations from purring seem to be good for healing wounds, lessening pain, and helping bones grow. But house cats are not the only animals that purr. Hyenas, raccoons, and guinea pigs also purr.

Q How do bats see in the dark?

Q

How do bats see in the dark?

Bats "see" with their ears.

Bats use their excellent sense of hearing to find their way in the dark and to avoid bumping into things. As they fly, bats let out very high-pitched squeaks or clicks. These sound waves strike nearby objects and bounce back, guiding the bats in flight. Using sound to find things in the dark is called **echolocation**. Bats that hunt at night for insects use echolocation to find their next meal.

Q Why do elephants swing their trunks?

19

Elephants swing their trunks to pick up smells.

Elephants wave their trunks—the largest noses in the world—to collect **odors** from the air and ground. Their trunks sway back and forth to sniff other elephants and learn whether or not they are members of the herd. Elephants also lift their trunks high in the air to pick up smells from far away. With their trunks raised, elephants can locate distant sources of water or **identify** possible dangers.

Q Do whales breathe underwater?

No, whales breathe air like other mammals.

Whales are mammals, not fish. Like other mammals, whales have lungs to breathe air. Since they live in the ocean and swim underwater, whales must come up to the surface to breathe from time to time. The air enters and leaves through nostrils, called blowholes, on top of the whale's head. Breathing out forms a cloud, called a spout, which is mostly water vapor. Some whale spouts can reach as high as a three-story building!

Q Why do wolves howl?

Howling keeps the wolf pack together.

Wolves often howl on their own or together with other members of their pack. Because they wander far and wide to find food, wolves often get separated from one another. Howling is the best way to find fellow pack members and stay in touch. Howling also helps a wolf pack mark its territory and keep other packs away. When two packs meet, the larger pack usually howls loudly to show off its greater size.

Q Why do opossums play dead?

Opossums act dead to escape danger

When threatened, an opossum drops to the ground, drooling with its mouth open and its tongue out. A foul-smelling green liquid oozes from its unmoving body. To anyone around, the opossum looks and smells as though it is dead and **decaying**. Dogs, foxes, coyotes, owls, and other predators are not tempted to eat it, so they leave. Once the coast is clear, the opossum "comes back to life."

Q Are apes a type of monkey?

No, apes and monkeys are different kind of animals.

Although often confused, apes and monkeys are different in many ways. Perhaps most obvious, apes do not have tails like monkeys. Also, apes are generally larger and heavier than monkeys. When compared to monkeys, apes have bigger brains and they are usually smarter. Because of their greater size and heavier bodies, apes spend more time on the ground than monkeys, who mostly live in trees.

Q Why do lions have manes?

Manes make lions look larger and scarier.

An adult male lion can be recognized by the mane of hair around its head. The mane makes the lion look more threatening, which can protect it from being attacked by an enemy. A heavy mane seems to signal to attackers that the lion is healthy, strong, and tough—and that the attacker should stay away. Perhaps most important, a mane helps a lion find a mate. Lionesses seem to prefer males with long, dark manes.

Q Why do rabbits wiggle their noses?

Wiggling noses help rabbits detect odors in the air.

Rabbits always seem to be wiggling, or twitching, their noses. That's because they depend on their **keen** sense of smell to pick up even the weakest of odors. Twitching alerts them to any threat of danger. When frightened or excited, a rabbit may twitch its nose 120 times a minute. However, when calm and safe, the rabbit may slow its twitching to only 20 times a minute or even stop altogether.

Q

Can chimps talk?

No, chimps can't talk, but they do communicate.

Chimpanzees can grunt, bark, hoot, scream, and make many other sounds, but they cannot use their vocal cords to speak in a way that humans can understand. Scientists in recent years have studied chimp communication and taught them American Sign Language (ASL). Scientists now believe that chimps can learn to understand the meaning of words—even though they cannot talk as humans do.

Q Are cheetahs the fastest mammals?

Yes, cheetahs are the fastest mammals over short distances.

When chasing **prey**, cheetahs can reach top speeds of up to 70 miles per hour (112 kph), but only for about 1,000 feet (300 m). That makes the cheetah faster than any human runner or race horse! As the cheetah zips along, its **flexible** spine bends up and down, letting it take *very* long strides. Large paws and claws act like cleats, gripping the ground firmly, and the cheetah's huge nostrils and lungs take in extra oxygen for super power.

Mud keeps pigs cool and protects their skin.

Pigs like to roll in mud when temperatures are high. Turning over and around in big puddles of mud helps pigs cool off in hot weather. While bathing in water also lowers their temperature, sloshing in mud keeps a pig cooler for longer. Mud is also a kind of sunscreen that protects a pig's delicate pink skin from the sun's powerful rays. At the same time, the mud protects the animals from harmful insects.

Q Do porcupines shoot their quills?

No, porcupines
can't shoot
their quills.

Porcupines use their **quills** to protect themselves
from enemies. However, they don't shoot their
quills at predators, as once believed. A frightened
porcupine jumps at its enemy or brushes up against
it. This drives a number of sharp, spiky quills into the
enemy's fur or flesh. Or, the porcupine may smack an
enemy with its quill-covered tail, causing great pain
and discomfort. One way or another, enemies quickly
learn not to attack porcupines.

Q

Why do dogs pant?

41

Panting helps dogs stay cool.

When dogs get hot, they can't cool off by sweating, like humans do. Unlike people, dogs have almost no sweat glands and are covered with warm, hairy coats! So, they pant by hanging their tongue outside their mouth and breathing quickly. Panting dries the **saliva** from the dog's tongue and mouth, which cools the blood that circulates to its lungs and helps lower its body heat. A dog that hangs its tongue out after running is just letting off steam!

20 BONUS FACTS

1 Giraffes have only seven neck bones—the same as you!

2 Dolphin brains weigh more than human brains!

3 No two zebras look exactly alike because every zebra has its own pattern of stripes!

4 Horses can stand on their feet for up to three years without tiring.

5 A camel's hump can weigh up to 80 pounds (36 kg)!

6 Big cats that roar, such as lions and tigers, cannot purr!

7 A single brown bat can catch 1,200 insects in an hour!

8 Bears can sleep for more than one hundred days without eating or drinking!

9 The trunk of an adult elephant is about six feet (1.8 meters) long.

10 A whale can hold its breath for as long as two hours underwater!

11 Wolves howl at different pitches to make the pack seem larger.

12 An opossum can play dead for up to four hours.

13 Apes' arms are longer than their legs; monkeys' arms are the same length or shorter than their legs.

14 Some male lions in the hottest climates have no manes at all.

15 A rabbit's nose twitches even while the rabbit is asleep.

16 Chimpanzees that know ASL can use it to communicate with other chimps, as well as with humans.

17 African elephants are the largest land mammal in the world.

18 Pigs like to wallow in mud, but they keep their nests very clean.

19 Each porcupine has about 30,000 quills.

20 A dog's only sweat glands are on the pads of its paws.

GLOSSARY

Color-blind – unable to tell certain colors apart

Decaying – the slow rotting or breaking down of plants or animals

Flee – to run away, especially from danger

Flexible – able to bend

Herds – large groups of animals

Hibernate – to sleep for an entire winter

Identify – to tell what something is

Keen – sharp or excellent

Mammals – animals that have backbones, hair, care for their young and nurse them with mother's milk, have a larger brain than other animals, and have a temperature that stays about the same no matter their surroundings

Mass - a large amount of something

Odors - smells

Predator - an animal that hunts and eats other animals

Prey - an animal that is hunted or eaten by other animals

Quills - long, hard, pointed bristles on a porcupine's skin made up of hairs that have grown together

Rivals - animals that compete against one another

Saliva - the liquid found in the mouth that keeps it moist and helps digestion

Scarce - hard to get or find

Threatened - afraid that something dangerous is about to happen

INDEX